The Kids' Book of
FRIENDS
How to Make Friends and Be a Friend

Copyright @WoodenHouseBooks, 2023.
Catherine and Jenny Stephenson
Illustrator: Hiruni Kariyawasam

All rights reserved
979-8363261220
First impression, 2023
Wooden House Books
www.woodenhousebooks.com

A note for grown-ups

This book helps children practice real friendship skills, at home, at school, and in everyday play.

- ⭐ **Meeting and joining in**
  Ideas for saying hello and joining play

- ⭐ **Kind friend skills**
  Taking turns, listening, and being thoughtful

- ⭐ **Fixing friendship bumps**
  What to do after a mistake or argument

- ⭐ **Brave boundaries**
  What to do when something feels unfair

- ⭐ **When your child feels left out**
  Comforting ideas and next steps

- ⭐ **Gentle practice pages**
  Draw, circle, and talk together

Tip: Read in any order. Choose a page that fits your child's day.

This Friends book belongs to
_____

Friends can be awesome!

Friends can be awesome! There are lots of people in the world... but only some become real friends.

In this book, we'll explore:

- How do we make a friend?

- What makes friends special?

- What if things change?

Let's follow Frida and Freddie to find out!

A friend is someone who...

A friend makes you smile.

A friend helps you feel safe.

A friend likes you
just the way you are.

Friends can be different and still be friends!

Friends can be different from you. They might look different, talk differently, or like other things.

Some friends are quiet. Some friends are super silly.

You can be friends with anyone who is kind and makes you feel welcome.

Making a friend starts with hello.

FIRST STEP

When you want to make a friend, start with a hello. You can smile, wave, or ask, "Want to play?"

"Hi!"

If they're not ready, that's okay. You can try again later, or say hello to someone else.

Here are some friendly things you can say to someone new.

- That game looks fun.
- Do you want to build something?
- Hi! Want to play together?
- Can I sit with you?
- What's your favorite color?
- I like your hat!

Feeling shy?

- Can I watch?
- Can I have a turn next?

⭐ Say hello to someone new. What could you say?

What do you both like?

Friends often like some of
the same things.
Maybe you both like trains...
dancing... or dinosaurs!
You can ask questions
and find out.

Inviting others to play.

If you see someone on their own, you can smile, wave, and ask, "Want to play with us?

Want to join our game?

Freddie saw a child sitting alone.
"Want to join our game?" he asked.
The child smiled. "Okay," they said, and came along.

One kind invitation can start a new friendship. ♥

Friends show kindness.

Kindness is one of the best ways to be a friend.

GROW

At snack time, Frida noticed Xiao looked sad.

She gently asked, "Want to talk?" Then she smiled and sat beside her.

⭐ Can you think of something kind someone did for you?

Friends share and take turns.

Sometimes we both want the same thing, like a toy, a game, or a turn.

Friends take turns so everyone gets a chance.

Freddie really wanted to go first.

But he let Ellie roll the dice.

They took turns, and laughed when Ellie slid down a big snake!

Freddie played with his puzzle cube. Leo watched.

"Want a turn?" asked Freddie.

Leo smiled. "Yes, please!"

They took turns and laughed.

Friends can use kind words.

⭐ Try one kind word today. Which will you pick?

Friends can be themselves
with each other.

Freddie loved dressing up like a dinosaur. His friend roared too, and they had a dino parade.

It's always okay to be you!

A good friend makes you feel safe and happy just as you are.

Friends can be loyal.

Friends are loyal. They stay with you and help you, even when things are hard.

If others laugh, a loyal friend doesn't join in.

Noa fell over and some kids laughed.

Frida did not laugh. She ran over and helped her up.

"Are you okay?" she asked. Noa nodded. She felt a little braver.

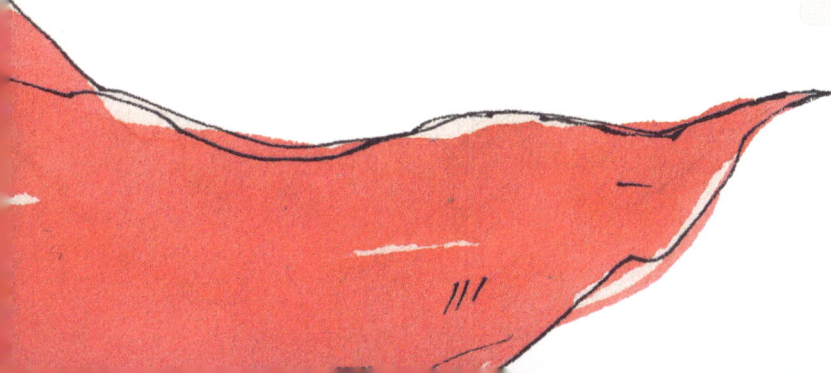

Friends can help each other.

Listening and paying attention shows you care.

If your friend feels sad, you can sit with them.

Try saying:

Do you want help?

Are you okay?

I can help you.

Ben dropped his things. Freddie asked, "Are you okay?"
Then he helped Ben pick them up.

A little help can mean a lot.

Friends argue sometimes.

Freddie wanted to play his game. Millie wanted to play hers.

They shouted.
They turned away.
Nobody was having fun anymore.

FIX

Friends can want different things. A short break can help.

When you're ready, try saying:

> I didn't like that. Can we try again?
>
> I'm sorry. Next time I'll use a calm voice.
>
> Can we take turns?
>
> Can we make a plan?

It's okay to make mistakes.

Later, Freddie said, "I'm sorry I yelled."

Millie nodded. "I'm sorry too."

They smiled. Then they started again, together.

Feeling left out.

REPAIR

NAME IT

Sometimes you might feel left out. That can feel sad or lonely.
It is not your fault.

TRY WORDS

You can ask to join. Try one of these. Pick the one that feels right.

GET HELP

Sometimes a game is full. But if it feels unkind, or keeps happening, tell a trusted grown-up.

Kind hands.

Sometimes friends play too rough.

If your body doesn't like it, you can say "Stop."

You deserve kind hands and kind words.
You can be kind and still say no.

If someone is too rough, you can use brave words:

Stop words
Stop. I don't like that
Please stop
I said stop

Body/boundary words
Gentle hands, please
Don't touch my body, please
That's too rough.

Exit words
I need space
I'm going to play over here

If they don't stop, **move** away and tell a grown-up you trust.

Friends don't need to be together all the time.

Frida loves reading.

Her friend Jada loves playing ballgames.

Sometimes they play together. And sometimes they play apart. They're still friends.

It's okay to do your own thing.

You can play alone or with others.

Different friends make life more fun.

Be a friend to yourself.

Talk to yourself kindly. Just like you would to a friend.

⭐ Today I can tell myself:

You can whisper it, or say it in your head.

Kind words can help.
Here are some you can try:

I am learning.

I am brave.

I can do hard things.

I can try again.

⭐ Which kind words will you choose today?

If your feelings still feel too big, tell a grown-up you trust.

Friends sometimes change.

That can feel sad.

Friends can change as you grow.
Someone might move away.
You might like new things.
That's okay.

I missed my friend and felt shy.

At the park, a kid smiled and said, "Want to slide?" We whooshed down together.

My shy feeling got smaller.

You can miss a friend and still make a new one.

Friendship toolbox.

When you're not sure what to say, try one of these.

Pick one. Try it. That's brave.

HELLO STARTERS

Hi! Want to play?

Can I join you?

What are you playing?

BRAVE BOUNDARIES

Stop. I don't like that.

Please give me space.

That's not okay.

REPAIR WORDS

I didn't like that. Can we try again?

I'm sorry.

Next time I will...
- ☐ use a calm voice
- ☐ take turns ☐ ask first

WHEN I FEEL LEFT OUT

Can I play too?

Is there room for me?

Okay. Can I play next time?

♥ If it keeps happening, tell a grown-up you trust.

Friendship is built from small moments: hello, sharing, taking turns, being kind.

Some friendships begin today.

Some grow a little every day.

Take your time.

A hello is enough to start.

Friendship grows little by little.

It starts with being you.

And you are enough. 🩷

Want to practice? Turn the page!

Want to practice friendship skills?
Try these fun pages with a grown-up.

Friendship Games

Friendly foxes.

Being friendly can help you make friends.

Try these ideas. Add your own too!

- Ask them questions about what they like
- Wave to them when you see them out and about.
- Share your toys and snacks
- Say kind things to them.
- Smile and say hi.
- Ask them if they want to play with you.
- Tell them about your favorite games and places to go
- Think of a different game to play if they don't like the same one as you.

Emotion detectives.

Be an emotion detective.
How do you feel inside?

Now look at the faces.
Match the feeling words to the right face.

_ Happy
_ Angry
_ Upset
_ Excited
_ Silly
_ Surprised

Making faces.

Your face can show your feelings.

Other people's faces can give you clues too.

Draw a face for each feeling.

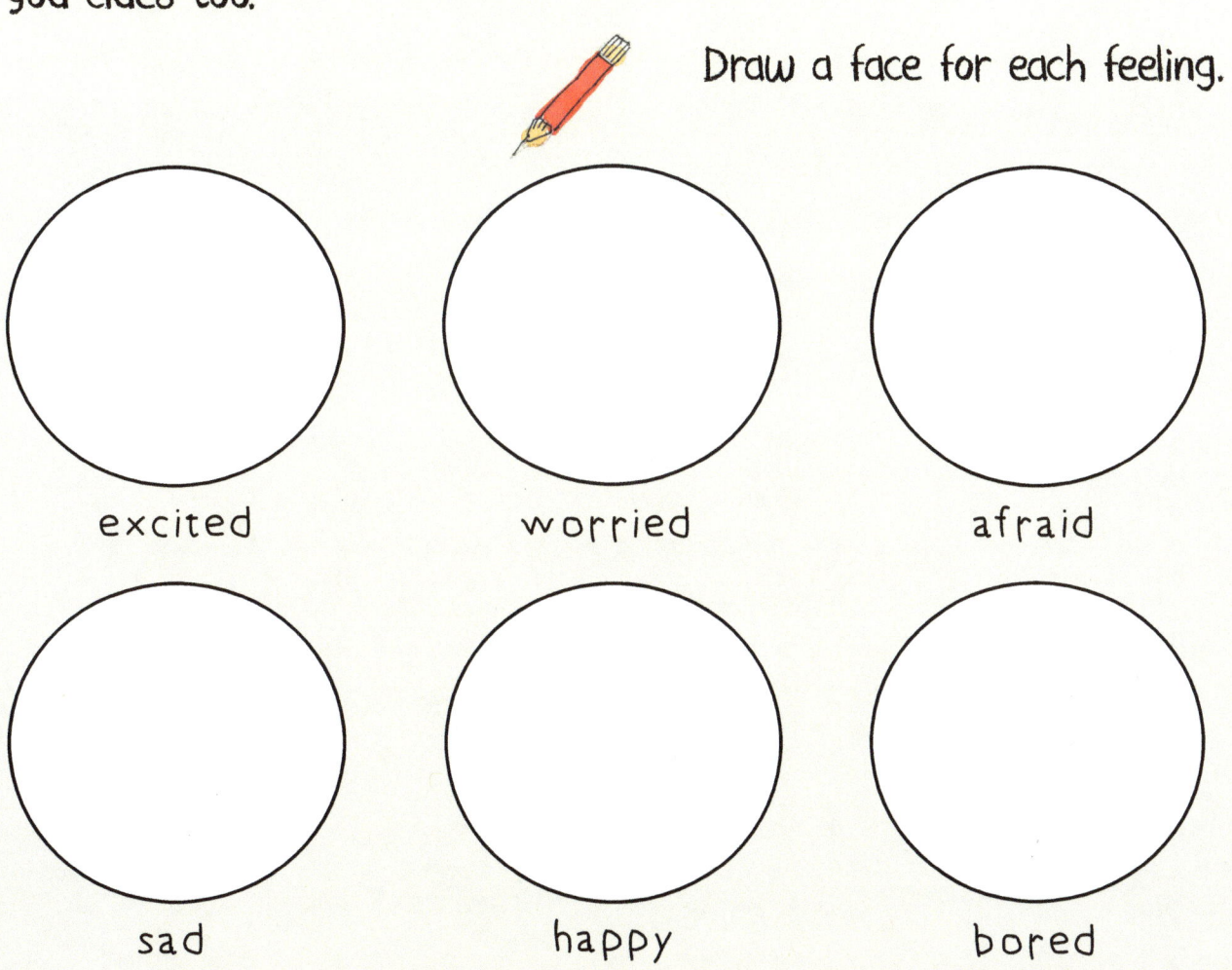

Kind words.

What kind words have people said to you? What kind words can you say to others?

Write some kind words in the bubbles

Friendship flower.

Everyone has special qualities that make them a good friend.

Draw your face in the middle (or write your name).
On each petal, write one good friend quality.

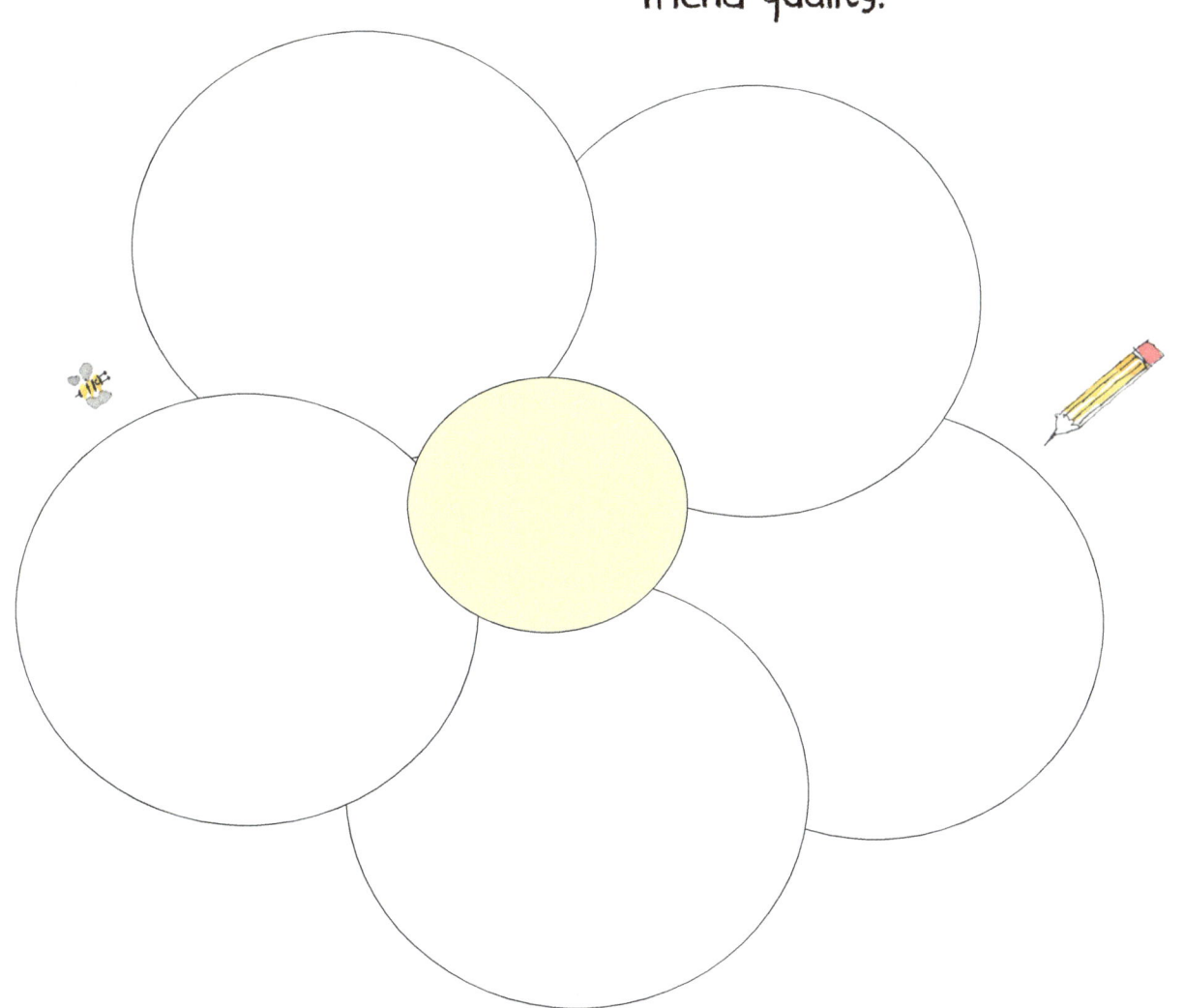

From Our Family To Yours.

Thank you for spending time with this book.
We hope it was helpful for your family.

If you have a moment, please leave a quick review on Amazon.

Even a short rating or a few words helps other families find this book and helps our small team keep creating resources for children.

Many thanks for your support.

With care,
The Wooden House Books family 🩷

Say hello to the Wooden House Books team.

Gentle books that help children learn and grow.

Catherine • Author

Catherine grew up in Wales and now lives in Barcelona with her family and two cats. She's a writer and translator from Spanish and Catalan into English, and she loves writing children's books. She has also taught English to children.

Hiruni • Illustrator

Hiruni is from Ambalangoda, Sri Lanka. She studied Fashion Design at the University of Moratuwa and now illustrates full-time. She creates warm, playful children's book art using pencil and watercolour.

Jenny • Educational Psychologist

Jenny is a chartered educational psychologist in the UK. She supports children, families, and schools with practical tools for learning, wellbeing, and calmer days. She works with Brighter Futures and runs HappySleepers, helping children sleep well.

WOODEN HOUSE BOOKS

Also in the Wooden House Books collection:

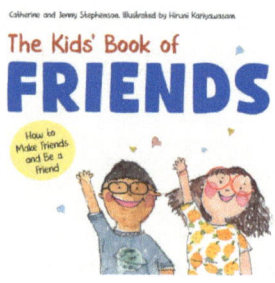
Friends
Ages 3-7

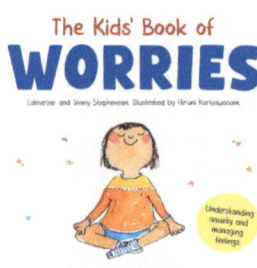
Worries
Ages 4-9

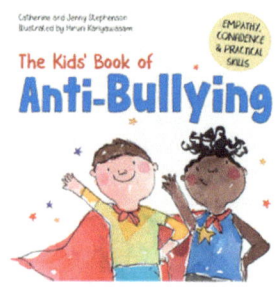
Bullying
Ages 4-8

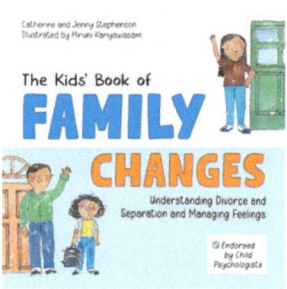
Family changes
Ages 6-10

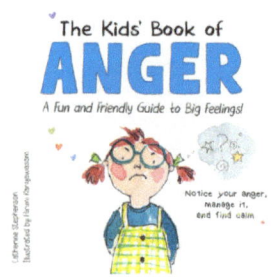
Anger
Ages 4-8

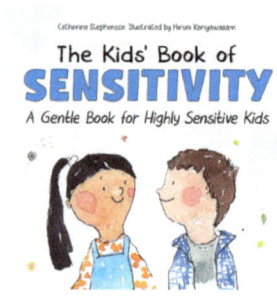
Sensitivity
Ages 4-10

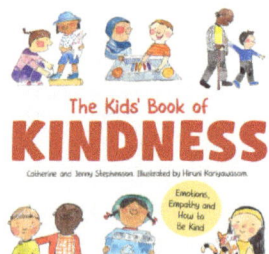
Kindness
Ages 3-8

Emotions
Ages 4-9

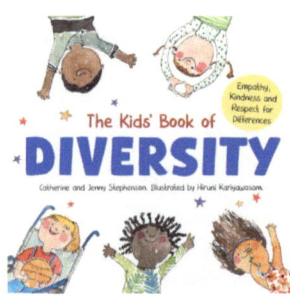
Diversity
Ages 3-8

Get your free friendship and kindness resource!

Looking for more gentle ways to support social-emotional learning?

Download a free 9-page printable PDF with simple friendship and kindness activities for children – plus occasional thoughtful updates from Wooden House Books.

Small moments. Real learning.

www.woodenhousebooks.com

or scan the QR code below:

Scan for your free download

Print and go • Ages 3-7
(Ideal for ages 4-6)

Little Friendship Moments
Fun, Kind Activities for Kids!

Inside you'll find friendly moments about:
- 💛 Kindness
- 😊 Saying hello
- 🤝 Taking turns
- 🌈 Helping others
- ⭐ Being yourself

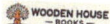

Want to keep growing your friendship skills?

Don't miss The Kids' Book of Friends Activity Book!

With **35 fun activities**, kids:

- Practice kindness and empathy
- Learn how to join in and make friends
- Solve small problems and make up
- Celebrate what makes each friendship special

It's a fun, hands-on way to make, keep, and enjoy friendships. Find it on Amazon and keep building friendship skills!

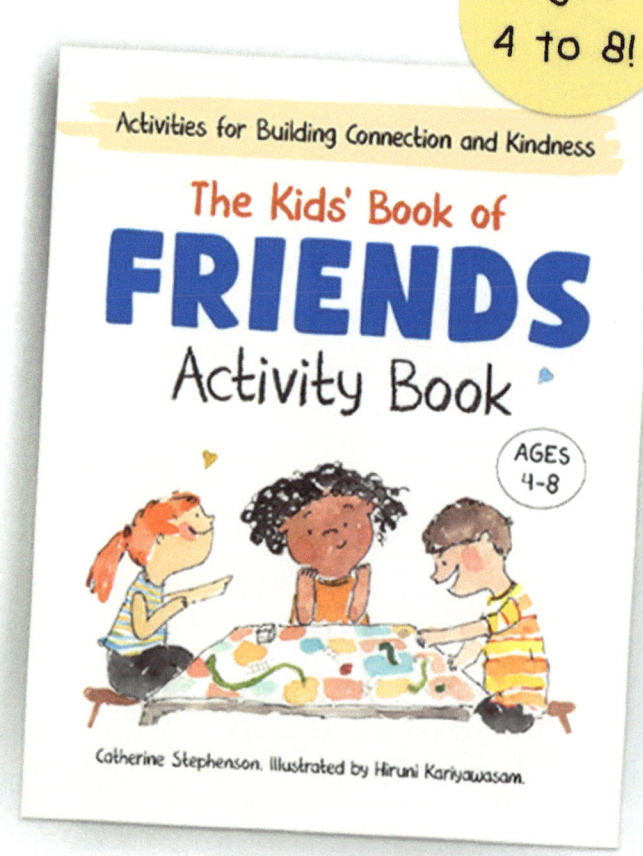

www.ingramcontent.com/pod-product-compliance
Lightning Source LLC
Chambersburg PA
CBHW042248100526
44587CB00002B/65